W0007298

The Human Body
Explained to Kids

Discover the Fascinating Secrets and Wonders of Your Body

Coordinator: Kavya Sharma

Writers: Kavya Sharma, Morgan Barrett, Anne Moore, Juan Rodriguez

Illustrators: Mary Banks, Aryan Patel, Ming-Hui Zhang, iStock

Table of Contents

Embark on an Epic Journey through the Vast Wonders of the Universe!

Uncover the mysteries of the different planets, galaxies, and celestial bodies that make up our universe.

With this book, you'll unravel the secrets of the universe that surrounds us.

So, if you're ready to explore the wonders beyond our world, check out "The Universe Explained to Kids"!

Introduction

Welcome, brave explorer! You're about to set off on the most exciting journey of your life - right inside your own body.

Think of your body as a gigantic city, full of hustle and bustle. It's like a well-oiled machine, where every little part, every tiny citizen has a special job to do. In this city, you are the captain. You are the hero!

There are super-highways known as veins, there are pumping stations like the heart, and there's even a command center, your brain. There are factories like your stomach that turn food into energy. Some parts are solid like your bones, others are squishy like your lungs, and some are teeny-tiny like the cells.

Everywhere you look, something amazing is happening. It's a never-ending festival of life, happening right inside you, every moment of every day.

In the tiniest corner to the grandest organ, each bit of you is a treasure with a story to tell.

Ready to dive in? Grab your explorer's hat, and let's zoom into this amazing world that is YOUR BODY! Are you ready for this adventure?

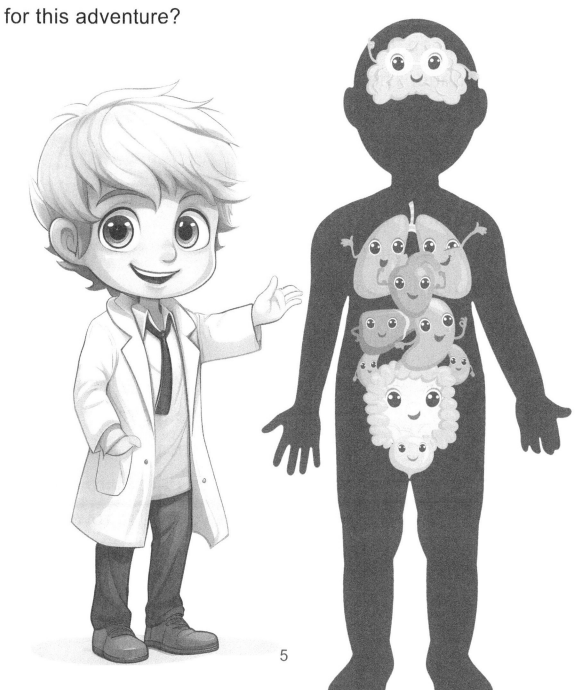

~ The Skin ~

Have you ever felt the thrill of a cool breeze on your face or the tickle of grass under your feet? It's all thanks to your incredible skin! Your skin is like a magical cloak that covers your entire body, protecting everything inside.

Inside your incredible skin, three special layers work together to keep you safe and sound. The outermost layer is called the epidermis, and it's like a tough shield that protects you from harm. It keeps germs out and helps you feel things like a tickle or a touch.

Right below the epidermis, we have the dermis, which is like a strong fortress. It has tiny blood vessels, nerves, and even hair follicles (these are little pockets where your hair grows from). The dermis helps your skin stay healthy and gives it its strength.

Deep down, we find the hypodermis, a layer of fat that acts as a cozy cushion. It helps keep your body warm and stores extra energy for you to use. Together, these three layers make up your incredible skin, working like a team to keep you safe, healthy, and ready for adventures!

And here's a special secret about your skin: It loves the sun! When the sun shines on your skin, it helps your body make a special vitamin called vitamin D. Vitamin D makes your bones strong and healthy. But remember, too much sun can be harmful to your skin. So when you go outside to play, make sure to wear a hat and use sunscreen to protect your amazing skin.

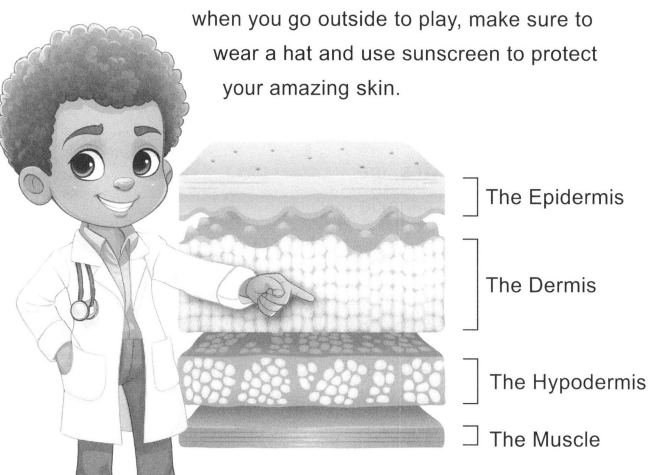

The Epidermis

The Dermis

The Hypodermis

The Muscle

~ Freckles and Nevi ~

In the wondrous realm of the human body, there exist two captivating characters: freckles and nevi. Let us embark on a thrilling adventure to uncover the secrets they hold.

Freckles, those whimsical specks of magic, are like gentle kisses from the sun. They appear on your skin, creating a playful dance of dots. Melanin, the special pigment artist within your body, creates these sun-kissed wonders. When the sun's rays touch your skin, melanocytes, the color-making cells, sprinkle freckles across your cheeks, nose, and arms.

But wait, there's more to our tale! Enter the nevi, mysterious marks that decorate your skin. They come in various shapes, sizes, and colors, like tiny treasures waiting to be discovered. Nevi, also known as moles, birthmarks, or beauty marks, are like hidden stories etched onto your canvas.

These enigmatic marks are made by clusters of pigment cells called melanocytes. Sometimes, they are born with you, like a special gift from the universe. Other times, they appear as you grow, creating new tales with each passing year.

While some nevi are small and shy, others may grow larger or change over time. Like unique fingerprints, they make you truly one-of-a-kind. Remember, just like the stars in the sky, nevi are meant to be admired and protected.

So, as you explore the magical world of your body, embrace freckles and nevi. Cherish these celestial markings, for they make you uniquely magnificent, inside and out.

~ Acne ~

Deep beneath the surface of your skin, there's a bustling city called the "pores." And in this city, there's an intriguing character called the sebaceous gland, who loves to create a thrilling spectacle known as acne!

The sebaceous gland's job is to produce a special oil called sebum, which keeps your skin soft and moisturized. But sometimes, this gland gets carried away and produces too much sebum, causing trouble in the city of pores.

Picture tiny construction workers toiling away inside the pores, building houses with dead skin cells. However, when too much sebum is around, these workers get stuck, blocking the way and creating a traffic jam. It's like a mini-adventure beneath your skin!

The trapped dead skin cells and sebum create a cozy environment for another resident, the bacteria. They feast on the excess sebum and multiply rapidly, leading to an army of red and inflamed soldiers on your skin called pimples.

Acne can show up on your face, back, or chest, and sometimes it likes to make a dramatic entrance during your teenage years. But fear not, young adventurer! With proper care and a little patience, you can defeat these pesky pimples.

Remember to wash your face gently, keep your skin clean, and avoid touching your face too much. Soon, the bustling city of pores will calm down, and your skin will once again glow with happiness!

~ Sweat ~

Sweat is like the body's natural cooling system. It's a watery liquid that comes out of our skin when we get hot or do exercise. Just like when you run around and your body starts to feel warm, sweat helps to cool you down.

Sweat comes from special glands in our skin called sweat glands. These glands are like tiny factories that make and release sweat. They work hard to keep our bodies at a comfortable temperature.

Drinking water and seeking shade when necessary will help maintain your body's equilibrium and keep you safe during your heroic endeavors.

Did you know that we all have millions of sweat glands all over our bodies? Some areas, like our armpits and forehead, have more sweat glands than others. That's why those places can feel sweatier sometimes.

But what's really special about sweat? Well, it's not just water. It's a clever mix of salt and water, a secret potion your body creates. As it drips away, sweat takes some of the heat with it, like a magical evaporating cloak.

When we sweat, it's usually odorless, which means it doesn't have a smell. But sometimes, sweat can smell a bit stinky. Do you know why? It's because of some special bacteria that live on our skin.

These bacteria like to eat the sweat that comes out of our skin. When they eat the sweat, they produce a substance that has a smell. So, the smell you might notice is actually from the bacteria, not the sweat itself. Keeping clean and fresh can help keep those smells at bay!

~ The Hair ~

In a world full of wonders, there exists something truly extraordinary—our hair! Look closely, and you'll find it growing on our heads, like a magnificent crown. But did you know that hair is more than just a pretty decoration? Let's embark on an exciting journey to discover the incredible functions of our hair.

First and foremost, hair is a mighty protector! It shields our delicate scalp from the blazing sun, just like a brave knight defending a castle. With its invisible armor, it keeps harmful ultraviolet rays at bay, ensuring our skin stays safe and healthy.

But that's not all! Our hair is a master at controlling temperature. Just imagine, when it's chilly outside, our hair acts like a cozy blanket, wrapping around our heads to keep warmth close. It's like having a cozy bonnet made of invisible threads!

And here's the fascinating part: our hair possesses an extraordinary power— the power of touch! Like tiny superheroes, certain hairs on our bodies, such as eyebrows and eyelashes, have a special mission. They act as super-sensitive sensors, detecting gentle touches, tickles, and even the tiniest breeze. It's as if they have tiny hands, whispering secrets of the world to our skin.

So, my young explorers, remember the marvelous hair that adorns our heads! Our hair is like a guardian angel, watching over us and making us feel special.

~ The Nails ~

Nails, my dear young explorers, are like tiny shields protecting our fingertips from harm. They are made of a substance called keratin, just like our hair. Did you know that your nails are actually dead cells? Yes, it's true! But they are very much alive at their base, called the nail bed, where the magic begins.

Every day, while you're playing and having fun, your nails are growing! They start growing from the root hidden beneath your skin. Isn't that amazing? Just like a plant, they need good food and care to flourish.

Here's a fun fact: Nails grow faster in the summertime! Maybe it's because they love the warmth of the sun. And

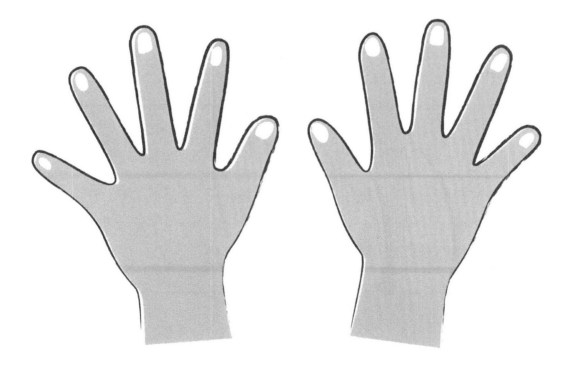

did you know that if you look
closely, you can see tiny
lines on your nails?
They're called
growth rings, and
they show how fast
your nails have been
growing.

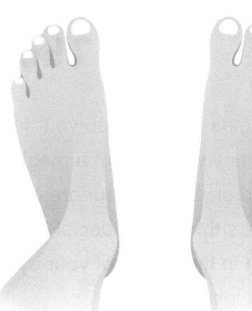

But nails aren't just pretty;
they have a crucial job too. They
help us pick up toys, hold pencils, and even scratch an
itchy nose. They are like our trusty assistants, always
ready to lend a hand.

So, my little adventurers,
next time you gaze at
your nails, remember
their extraordinary tale.
Keep them clean, keep
them strong, and let your
imagination soar as you
explore the world through the
wonders of your fingertips!

~ The Eyes ~

Imagine a window on your face, called the eye. It's not just any window, but a magical one that can capture and send pictures to your brain. The journey begins when light enters through a special opening called the pupil, located right in the center of your eye. It's like a tiny door that lets light inside.

Behind the pupil lies the colorful iris, a beautiful part of your eye. It's like a curtain that controls how much light enters, just like you adjust the brightness on your TV. The iris can be blue like the sky, green like grass, or even brown like a cozy tree trunk. Isn't that amazing?

Once the light passes through the pupil, it reaches the back of your eye, where the superpower lies—the retina! The retina is like a camera film, ready to capture all the exciting images. It works hard to transform light into messages that

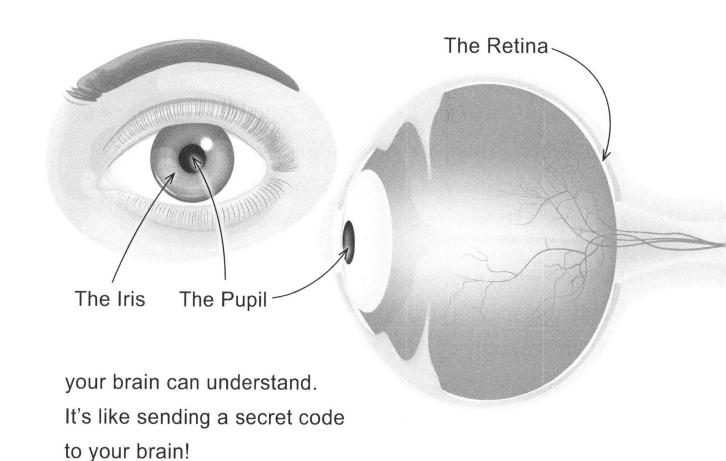

The Retina

The Iris   The Pupil

your brain can understand.
It's like sending a secret code
to your brain!

So, every time you see a beautiful
flower, a jumping bunny, or a
twinkling star, remember to
thank your incredible eyes.
They're like superheroes,
working together to bring
the magic of sight into your
world. Keep using your
superpower, little explorers,
and let your eyes guide you
through all the wonderful things
life has to offer!

~ The Tears ~

In a world of wonders, where our bodies hum with secrets, a captivating phenomenon emerges—tears. Picture the intricate machinery of your body, where tears play a remarkable role, far beyond what meets the eye.

The Lacrimal Gland

Nestled within your eyes lie the remarkable lacrimal glands, tirelessly working to produce these liquid marvels. When triggered by emotions or even irritants, such as onion vapors, these glands activate, setting in motion a chain reaction.

As tears form, they become an extraordinary concoction. This fluid blend comprises water and natural antibodies that help protect your delicate eyes from harm. But there's more to it than meets the eye.

Deep within your brain, a tiny structure called the hypothalamus acts as a conductor, orchestrating the

20

production of tears. When you experience intense emotions, this mastermind sends signals to the tear glands, igniting a complex process.

During this process, your tears release tiny helpers known as oxytocin and endorphins, which have extraordinary powers. Oxytocin, the "cuddle helper," creates feelings of warmth and connection, just like when you get a big hug from someone you love. Endorphins, your body's "feel-good helpers," are like a comforting blanket that makes you feel better when you're sad or in pain.

So, my young adventurer, embrace the magic of your tears. They are not merely drops of liquid, but intricate messengers carrying biological wonders. Shed tears when you need, for they bring comfort, strength, and a profound connection to the marvels that lie within.

~ The Ears ~

In a world of wonder, nestled on the sides of your head, live the marvelous ears! These magical organs help you hear all the amazing sounds around you. Let's embark on a thrilling journey to discover their secrets!

High up in your ears, a brave guardian stands tall—the eardrum. It's like a tiny drumskin that stretches across a tunnel called the ear canal. When sound waves come dancing through the air, they make the eardrum vibrate, just like a superhero's cape fluttering in the wind!

But the adventure doesn't stop there! Deep inside your ears lies the cochlea, a spiral-shaped treasure trove. This fantastic cochlea is like a snail's shell filled with thousands of tiny hairs. When the eardrum's vibrations reach this magical place, the hairs start to dance with joy!

Each hair in the cochlea has a special task: to transform sound into a language your brain can understand. They send signals to your brain like a secret message, telling it whether you're listening to a happy song, a chirping bird, or a friend's laughter.

Oh, the wonders of the ears! They help you hear the joyful melodies of birds, the rustling leaves in the wind, and the whispers of your loved ones. They allow you to dance to the beat of music and giggle at funny sounds. Your ears are like little heroes, always working together to bring sound into your world.

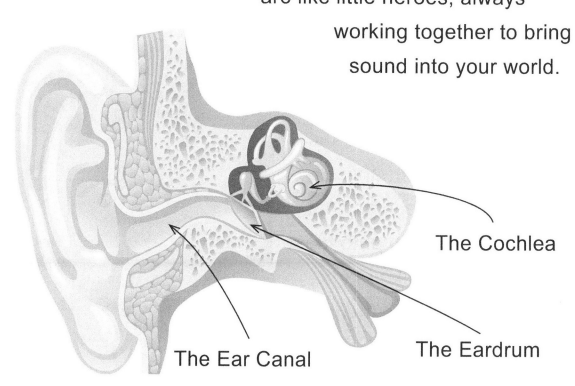

The Cochlea

The Ear Canal

The Eardrum

~ The Nose ~

In a world of smells and sniffs, there is one extraordinary hero – the nose! It sits right in the middle of your face, just above your mouth. The nose is like a detective, always sniffing out the mysteries of the world around us.

When you breathe in through your nose, the air takes a thrilling journey. It first enters your nostrils, those two little openings at the end of your nose. Inside your nose, there are special tiny hairs called cilia. They act as guardians, trapping dust and germs, keeping them from entering your body.

But that's not all! Your nose has an amazing power to smell. It has a super sense called olfaction. Tiny smell receptors line the inside of your nose, and when smelly molecules float in the air, they latch onto these receptors. Then, like magic, your brain interprets the smell, and you know if it's sweet like candy or stinky like socks!

But wait, there's more! The nose also has a secret weapon called mucus. When your nose produces mucus, it works hard to keep your nose clean and healthy. Sometimes, this mucus dries up and forms little solid bits that you may also hear being called "boogers." You might even know it as "snot." So, if you ever notice these little boogers or snot in your nose, don't worry! They're just a natural part of how your body keeps your nose free from dust and germs.

So next time you smell a fresh flower or detect a delicious pizza, remember to thank your nose. It's a remarkable part of your body, always ready to sniff out the exciting scents of the world.

~ The Mouth ~

Nestled within your face, lies a remarkable gateway to adventure—the incredible mouth! Like a brave knight guarding a castle, your mouth protects you from harm while embarking on the most daring quests.

The mouth is a fantastic fortress lined with sturdy soldiers called teeth. There are different types of teeth, each with its own special job. At the front of your mouth, you'll find the sharp incisors, just like little swords, helping you bite into tasty apples and carrots. Behind them, the strong and flat molars and premolars work together to grind and chew your food into tiny pieces.

But the magic doesn't stop there! Your mouth is a wonderland of secrets, hiding a powerful potion known as saliva. This enchanted liquid, made by small factories called salivary glands, helps you taste and digest your food. With each bite, the saliva swoops in, turning dry bread into a soft, moist mash.

Saliva is like a team of friendly helpers, taking care of your mouth as you chew. It wets the food, making it slippery and easy to swallow. It also carries special messages from your taste buds to your brain, telling you if something is sweet like honey or sour like a lemon.

Remember, by brushing your teeth, watching out for sugary snacks, and drinking water, you become a tooth-saving hero! So, keep your mouth happy and your teeth strong, and you'll have a dazzling smile that shines like a star.

~ The Tongue ~

In the marvelous kingdom of your mouth, there resides a magnificent explorer known as the tongue! The tongue is like a fearless adventurer, always ready to discover new tastes and textures that make your mouth dance with delight.

The tongue is a wondrous organ, covered in tiny bumps called taste buds. These taste buds are like magical sensors that help you experience different flavors. They have superpowers! Some taste buds can detect sweetness, like when you savor a juicy strawberry. Others can detect sourness, like when you pucker up after tasting a lemon.

When you take a bite of your favorite food, the tongue is the first to meet it. With each delicious morsel, the taste buds awaken and send messages to your brain, telling it all about the flavors you're experiencing. It's like a secret language only you and your taste buds can understand.

But the tongue is not just about taste; it's also a fantastic helper for your mouth. It moves food around while you chew, making sure every piece gets a fair chance to meet the taste buds. It's like a skilled conductor leading a symphony of flavors inside your mouth!

The tongue is a versatile explorer, capable of helping you speak different languages, too. It dances and twists to form sounds that express your thoughts and feelings. It's your partner in communication, helping you share stories, sing songs, and laugh with joy.

~ The Larynx ~

In a land where words danced and songs soared, there lived a special hero called the Larynx. It resided high up in your throat, just above your chest, protecting and guiding your voice.

When you speak, the larynx springs into action, like a secret door opening. It has two tiny, stretchy bands called vocal cords that sit side by side. When you breathe, they stay apart, allowing air to flow freely. But when you want to speak or sing, they come together like magic, forming a bridge over the windpipe.

With a flicker of sound, air rushes through the narrow opening between the vocal cords, causing them to vibrate.

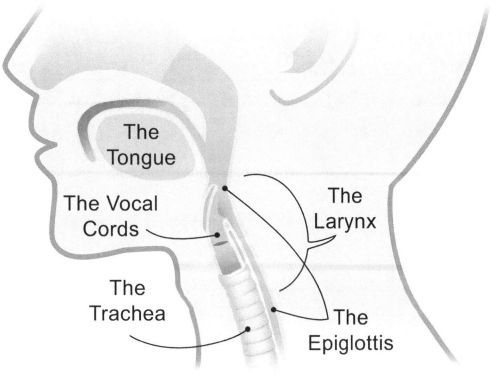

The Tongue

The Vocal Cords

The Trachea

The Larynx

The Epiglottis

This vibration creates sound waves, which travel up and out through your mouth, forming words and melodies. The larynx, with its mighty power, brings your voice to life!

But the larynx is not just a guardian of words; it's a protector too. When you swallow, a special flap called the epiglottis comes down, covering the larynx like a shield. It prevents food and liquids from entering your windpipe known as the trachea and going down the wrong way. The larynx keeps you safe and sound!

So, next time you speak or sing, remember the incredible larynx, the hero inside you. It helps you share your thoughts, express your feelings, and fill the world with joy. With the larynx on your side, there's no limit to the wonders your voice can create!

~ The Brain ~

In a world filled with wonders, one organ reigns supreme. It's the brain, a magnificent commander that helps you think, feel, and explore.

The brain is like a supercomputer, working nonstop to control everything you do. It helps you talk, walk, and play games. It even remembers your favorite ice cream flavor and how to tie your shoelaces!

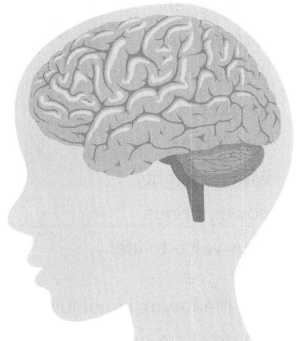

It's made up of billions of tiny cells called neurons. These special cells are the messengers of your thoughts, running through highways called nerves to different parts of your body.

When you see a colorful rainbow or taste a delicious chocolate chip cookie, it's your brain that's experiencing the magic. It captures all your senses and lets you enjoy the show.

But the brain is not just a watcher; it's also a master problem solver. When you face a puzzle or a tricky question, your brain springs into action. It thinks, plans, and finds clever solutions. It's like having a genius friend inside your head!

And that's not all! The brain is also a fantastic conductor of movement. It helps you jump, dance, and catch a ball. It's the maestro behind your motor control, making sure you move with grace and precision.

~ The Brainstem ~

The brainstem is like a brave guardian, standing tall at the base of your brain. It connects your brain to the rest of your body, just like a strong bridge. It controls vital functions that keep you alive and well, even while you sleep.

Imagine a control room filled with switches and buttons. That's the brainstem! It manages your breathing, heartbeat, and even your body temperature. It's like a conductor leading a symphony orchestra, ensuring that everything plays in perfect harmony.

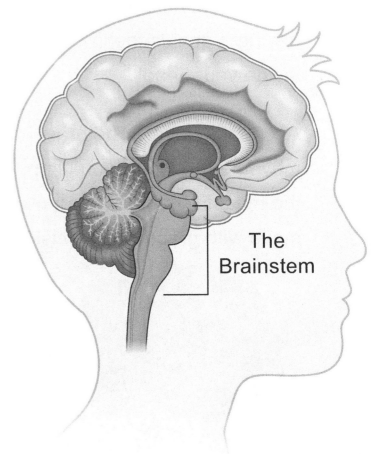

The Brainstem

When you're fast asleep, the brainstem whispers to your lungs, reminding them to take gentle breaths. It ensures your heart beats steadily, like a drum keeping rhythm. It's a tireless guardian, working day and night to keep you safe.

But that's not all! The brainstem also helps move and balance. It sends signals to your muscles, enabling you to jump, skip, dance with joy. It's like having a secret dance instructor who guides your every step.

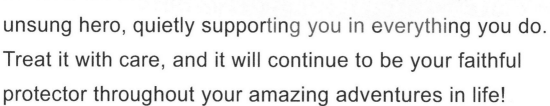

Next time you take a deep breath or hop on one foot, remember the mighty brainstem at work. It's the unsung hero, quietly supporting you in everything you do. Treat it with care, and it will continue to be your faithful protector throughout your amazing adventures in life!

~ The Neurons ~

In a world of wonder, inside your amazing body, a network of heroes awaits their moment to shine. Meet the mighty Neurons, the brave messengers of your body's commands!

Neurons are like tiny lightning bolts, sending messages at lightning speed. They have a special job: to carry information from one place to another. Imagine them as super-fast couriers, racing through your body to deliver important messages.

Dendrites

The Axon

Each neuron has a long, slender body with branches called dendrites. These branches reach out like trees in a magical forest, collecting messages from other neurons. When it's time to deliver the message, an electric spark travels down the neuron's body, guided by the axon, like a superhero on a mission.

But where do these messages go? They travel to the brain, the grand command center. Your brain, like a wise king, listens to each message and decides what needs to be done. It tells your body to move, to think, and to feel.

Neurons work together in incredible teams, forming a vast network called the nervous system. This system helps you do amazing things, like catch a ball, taste a sweet treat, or even giggle with joy.

~ The Heart ~

Prepare to be amazed as we dive into the captivating world of the human heart! Brace yourselves for an adventure like no other.

The Heart

Deep within your chest, lies a superstar organ called the heart. It's your body's very own drum, beating with rhythm and excitement. Can you feel your heart pounding in anticipation?

The heart is a mighty muscle, working day and night to keep you alive. It's like a superhero headquarters, pumping blood throughout your body. But did you know that the heart has its own special room? It's called the chest cavity, and it's like a cozy home for this incredible organ.

This powerhouse is about the size of your fist, but don't let its small size fool you! The heart is strong enough to squeeze blood out with every beat, sending it on a thrilling journey through a maze of tubes called blood vessels.

Did you know that your heart beats around 100,000 times every day? It's like a super-fast drummer inside your body!

So, my young adventurers, get ready for an exciting journey into the heart's secret world. In the next chapters, we'll uncover the heart's fantastic performance called the cardiac cycle.

This mesmerizing dance ensures that oxygen and nutrients reach every part of your body, making sure you have the energy to play, learn, and explore.

Remember, your heart is the beating drum of your body, so take a moment and listen to its magical rhythm. Your heart is truly a marvel!

~ The Cardiac Cycle ~
(Part 1)

In the incredible world of your body, there is a superstar organ called the heart. The heart has an important job: it pumps blood all around your body! Let's discover the thrilling journey of the cardiac cycle.

Imagine you're at a grand concert, waiting for the show to begin. The lights dim, and the curtains rise. Suddenly, the heart's symphony starts with a bang!

First, the curtains open, and the deoxygenated blood enters the right atrium **2** through the superior and inferior vena cava. The superior vena cava **1** brings deoxygenated blood from the upper body, including the head, neck, and arms, while the inferior vena cava **4** carries deoxygenated blood from the lower body, including the abdomen and legs.

The right atrium **2** fills up, getting ready for the next act.

Now, it's time for the show to really start! The curtains lift, and the right atrium contracts, pushing the blood into the right ventricle **5**. The tricuspid valve **3**, our loyal gatekeeper, opens wide to allow the blood passage.

Drumroll, please! The right ventricle **5** contracts, sending the blood through the pulmonary valve **6**. Like a rocket, the blood shoots into the pulmonary artery **7**, racing toward the lungs for a breath of fresh air.

This exhilarating adventure continues in Part 2...

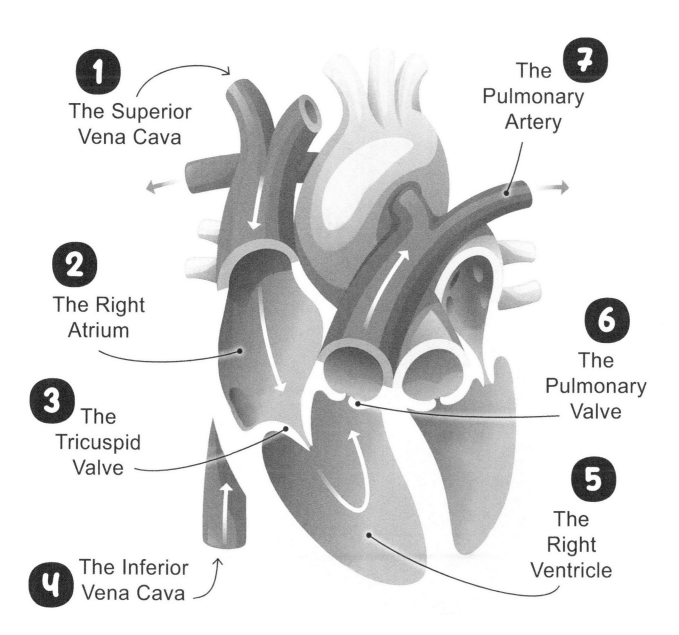

1 The Superior Vena Cava

2 The Right Atrium

3 The Tricuspid Valve

4 The Inferior Vena Cava

7 The Pulmonary Artery

6 The Pulmonary Valve

5 The Right Ventricle

~ The Cardiac Cycle ~ (Part 2)

Welcome back to the heart's incredible journey! In this chapter, we'll witness the thrilling second act of the cardiac cycle.

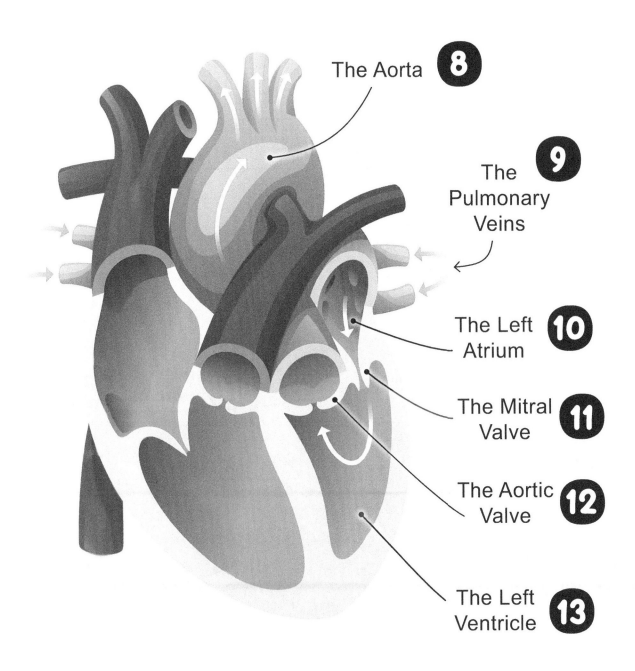

The Aorta **8**

The Pulmonary Veins **9**

The Left Atrium **10**

The Mitral Valve **11**

The Aortic Valve **12**

The Left Ventricle **13**

As we left off, the blood had just reached the lungs for a refreshing oxygen boost. Now, it's time for the oxygenated blood to return to the heart, like superheroes on a mission!

Through the pulmonary veins **9**, our courageous blood heroes enter the left atrium **10**, ready to continue their journey. The left atrium fills up, eagerly waiting for its cue.

Suddenly, the stage is set! The left atrium contracts, pushing the blood into the left ventricle **13**. The mitral valve **11** opens wide, inviting the blood inside.

The grand finale is about to begin! With a mighty push, the left ventricle contracts, squeezing the blood through the aortic valve **12**. It's like a strong gush of water from a fountain!

And off they go! The oxygenated blood zooms into the aorta **8**, the highway of our body. The aorta carries the blood to every nook and cranny, delivering precious oxygen and nutrients to our muscles, organs, and brain.

What an exhilarating journey! The heart's heroic performance in the cardiac cycle keeps us alive and full of joy. Take a moment to feel your own heartbeat and appreciate this remarkable symphony playing inside you. Bravo, heart, bravo!

~ The Blood Vessels ~

In the marvelous world inside your body, there are secret passages called blood vessels! They are like amazing highways that carry a special liquid called blood. Arteries, veins, and capillaries are the superheroes of these pathways, each with their unique powers!

Arteries are like speedy messengers, racing away from your heart with oxygen-rich blood! They have strong walls, pumping the blood quickly to all your body parts, delivering energy and life. Think of them as mighty rivers flowing through your body, bringing all the good stuff to keep you strong and active!

Veins, on the other hand, are the valiant rescuers, bringing back used blood to your heart. They work hard to collect all the waste and old cells, making sure your body stays clean and healthy. Their walls are

The Heart

thinner, like gentle streams that guide the tired blood back to your heart for a fresh start!

But wait, there's more! Capillaries are the tiny heroes, connecting arteries and veins. They have the superpower of being extremely thin, like delicate threads that reach every corner of your body. Through their walls, oxygen and nutrients sneak into your tissues, while waste and carbon dioxide slip back into the blood to be carried away!

Together, these blood vessels form an incredible network, delivering life to every cell in your body. They tirelessly work day and night, keeping you strong and full of energy! So next time you feel your heart beating, remember the extraordinary adventures happening inside, with the amazing arteries, veins, and capillaries fighting for your health!

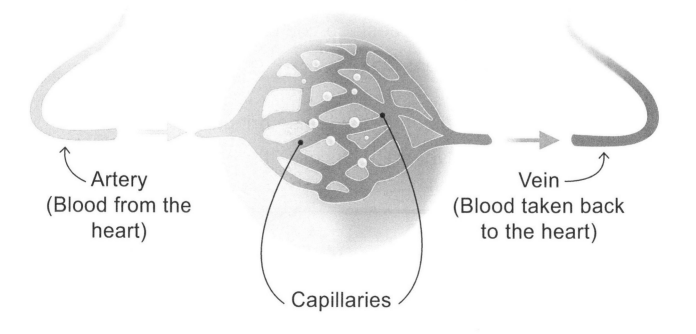

Artery
(Blood from the heart)

Vein
(Blood taken back to the heart)

Capillaries

~ The Blood ~

Deep within your body, there flows a mighty force called blood! It rushes through you, like a brave explorer on a thrilling quest. Imagine a bustling city with busy streets and tiny cars zooming around. Well, that's what your body looks like inside, and blood is the hero who keeps everything running smoothly.

Blood is made up of special cells called red blood cells, and they have a very important job. They carry oxygen, like a magical potion, to every part of your body. Blood carries oxygen from your lungs and spreads it to your muscles, bones, and even your brain. It helps them work their best, so you can run, jump, and think super fast!

But that's not all blood does! It also brings tasty nutrients to your body's cells. It's like a grand feast for your body! Blood travels through tiny tubes called blood vessels, just like the roads in a city, and delivers all the good stuff to every nook and cranny. It's like a food delivery service, ensuring that your body gets the energy it needs to grow strong.

Blood is a clever detective too! When your body is hurt, like when you get a cut or a scrape, blood rushes to the scene. It forms a special cover called a scab, like a protective shield, to keep germs away and help your body heal. It's like having your very own bodyguard, keeping you safe from harm.

So, inside you, a fearless team of superheroes fights battles every day. They deliver oxygen, bring nutrients, and protect your body from harm. Next time you feel your heart race or see a small scrape on your knee, remember that blood is always by your side, ready to keep you safe, strong, and full of energy!

~ White Blood Cells ~

Deep within your body, an army of brave warriors called White Blood Cells (or leukocytes) stands ready for battle! They are like the protectors of your body, always on guard against invaders. Imagine a castle with strong walls and courageous knights. Well, that's what your body looks like inside, and White Blood Cells are the mighty knights who keep you safe.

White Blood Cells have an important mission: to defend your body against germs and keep you healthy. They are like a secret task force, always on the lookout for trouble. When harmful germs try to sneak in, these valiant warriors jump into action!

Their first job is to surround and destroy the invaders. They have powerful weapons called enzymes that can break down germs. It's like a superhero battle where White Blood Cells defeat the bad guys.

But that's not all! They are also like clever detectives, searching for danger. When they find an enemy, they call for reinforcements. Other White Blood Cells rush to the scene, ready to fight. They work together like a united army, making sure no germ can take over your body.

White Blood Cells have a special power called "memory." Once they defeat an enemy, they remember it forever. So if that enemy tries to attack again, the White Blood Cells recognize it and defeat it quickly.

Next time you catch a cold, remember that your valiant warriors are hard at work, fighting for you!

~ Platelets ~

In the bustling world inside your body, where every part has a role to play, there are tiny heroes known as platelets (or thrombocytes). These mighty warriors are like the guardians of your body, always ready to protect you when you get a cut or a scrape.

Imagine you accidentally scrape your knee while playing. Ouch! Your body springs into action, sending the platelets on a daring rescue mission. These brave platelets race through your blood vessels like speedy race cars, zooming toward the injured spot.

Once they reach the scene, the platelets form a tight seal, just like a superhero putting up a shield. They stick together and create a special patch that stops the bleeding. This patch is called a clot. It acts like a protective bandage, preventing more blood from escaping.

But the platelets don't stop there. They call for reinforcements! Other heroes in your body, called red blood cells, rush to the scene to deliver oxygen and nutrients needed for healing. Together, they work as a team to mend your boo-boo and make it all better.

Platelets are small, but they have a crucial job. They help your body heal and keep you safe from harm. So next time you see a little cut, remember that the platelets are there, ready to spring into action and save the day!

~ The Bones ~

Imagine a super-strong scaffold that keeps you upright and protects your soft, delicate organs. That's right, bones are the sturdy pillars of your body! Located throughout your entire body, bones are like the secret warriors that help you stand tall and move around.

They form the framework that keeps everything in place. You can find bones in your arms, legs, skull, and even in your fingers and toes! Bones are made up of living cells that constantly work to grow and repair themselves.

Did you know that you have more than 200 bones in your body? But guess what? When you grow up, some of those bones fuse together, leaving you with 206 bones. It's like a magical puzzle!

The smallest bone in your body is called the stapes, and it's inside your ear. It's so tiny that it's about the size of a grain of rice! The stapes bone helps you hear all the fantastic sounds around you.

And do you want to know which bone is the biggest? It's the femur, located in the upper part of your leg, between your hip and your knee. The femur is like a mighty pillar that supports your whole body. It's as strong as an iron beam!

Bones also have a secret power—they store a special substance called calcium. It's like their own secret treasure! Calcium makes your bones strong and healthy, just like drinking milk does.

So, dear explorers, remember to take good care of your bones. Eat healthy foods, play and run, and always wear your helmet and knee pads when riding your bike or roller skating. Your bones will thank you for it, and you'll keep on adventuring for years to come!

~ The Muscles ~

Muscles are like stretchy rubber bands that surround your bones, giving you the ability to bend, twist, and turn. They're found all over your body, from your wiggly fingers to your jumpy toes. Some muscles are big and bulky, like the ones in your legs, while others are small and delicate, like the ones that help you smile.

But did you know, dear reader, that some muscles are so strong, they can pull with a force even mightier than a charging rhinoceros? Imagine that! It's like having your very own superhero inside your body. For instance, the jaw muscles that help you chew your favorite crunchy snacks are incredibly powerful. They can exert a force stronger than you can imagine!

Here's another fascinating fact: Muscles come in a variety of colors! Most muscles are a lovely shade of pink. But some muscles, like the heart, are a

vibrant and striking red, as if they're filled with the energy of a fiery volcano. And there are also muscles, such as the muscles in your arms and legs, that are a pure and glistening white.

So next time you wiggle your nose or wiggle your toes, remember to thank your muscles for being your body's mighty movers. They're always ready for action, keeping you strong and full of fun!

~ The Joints ~

In our amazing bodies, we have something very special called joints. Joints are like the superheroes of our bones, helping us move and play. They are the cool connectors that hold our bones together and allow us to bend, twist, and dance!

Imagine a door hinge, like the one on your bedroom door. Joints work just like that, but inside our bodies. They make sure our bones can swing open and close, just like a door! Isn't that incredible?

Whenever you jump, run, or even give a high-five, your joints are working hard. They let you reach up high in the sky or touch your toes down low. Without joints, we would be as stiff as statues, unable to move freely.

The Bone called "Femur"

The Patella
(The Kneecap)

The Joint of the knee

The Bone called "Tibia"

Joints are made up of amazing stuff! They have three main ingredients: cartilage, ligaments, and tendons.

Different joints do different jobs. Some joints, like your knees, help you walk and jump. Others, like your shoulders, help you throw a ball or hug someone tight. Each joint has a special purpose, and they all work together to make your body move and groove.

So, next time you wiggle your fingers, twist your hips, or wave your arms, remember to thank your joints for being awesome. They are the unsung heroes that make your body dance and play. Take care of your joints, and they will keep you moving and grooving for a long, long time!

~ The Tendons ~

Once upon a time, deep inside your body, there lived a group of extraordinary helpers called tendons. These mighty friends were like strong ropes, connecting your muscles to your bones. They were the true heroes behind every movement you made!

Imagine you are a superhero, ready to leap into action. Your tendons are your trusty sidekicks, ensuring your muscles and bones work together perfectly. When you kick a soccer ball, swing on a swing, or even jump for joy, it's all thanks to the magical power of tendons!

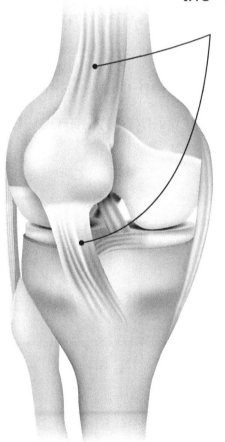

The Tendons of the knee

Tendons are like secret messengers, delivering messages from your brain to your muscles. They help your muscles pull on your bones, just like a puppeteer controlling a puppet. Whether you're running, skipping, or climbing, tendons keep you strong and stable.

Sometimes, though, tendons need extra care. Just like a knight wears armor, you should always protect your tendons by stretching and warming up before playing sports or doing exciting activities. They need to be strong and flexible to do their job well!

So, next time you wiggle your fingers, wiggle your toes, or wiggle your whole body, remember to thank your tendons. They are the quiet heroes inside you, ensuring you can move and explore the world around you. The tendons in your body are truly extraordinary!

~ The Ligaments ~

In a world of wondrous bodies, let's explore the amazing tale of the mighty ligaments! These invisible heroes, found throughout your body, are like the strong ropes that hold everything together.

Imagine you're a trapeze artist soaring through the air, performing daring flips and twists. Without ligaments, your bones would separate, causing you to crumble like a tower of blocks. Ligaments are like the trusty glue that connects bones, keeping them stable and allowing you to move with grace and strength!

But that's not all. These remarkable ligaments also protect your precious joints, like the hinges on a door. They wrap around your knees, elbows, and wrists, keeping them secure and preventing them from bending too far. So, the next time you jump, run, or even give a high-five, thank your ligaments for their steadfast support!

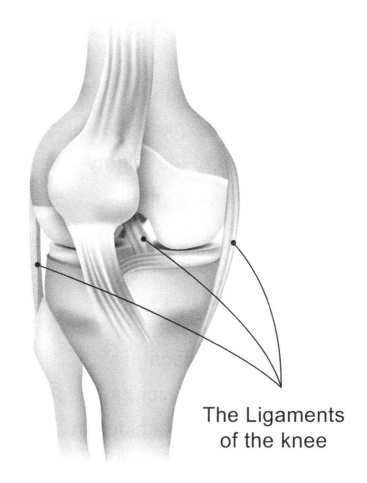

The Ligaments of the knee

Ligaments are like the heroes of your body, quietly working behind the scenes. They allow you to jump, twist, and explore the world around you. So, take care of them by eating healthy foods and staying active. By doing so, you'll keep your ligaments strong and ready for any adventure that comes your way!

Remember, dear readers, your ligaments are the champions that help you move and groove. They're the secret superheroes in your body, always there to lend a helping hand. So, embrace the magic of your ligaments and let them guide you on your wonderful journey through life!

~ The Cartilage ~

In a world of amazing wonders, let's explore the thrilling realm of the mighty cartilage! Brace yourself, young adventurers, as we journey into the incredible world of our bodies.

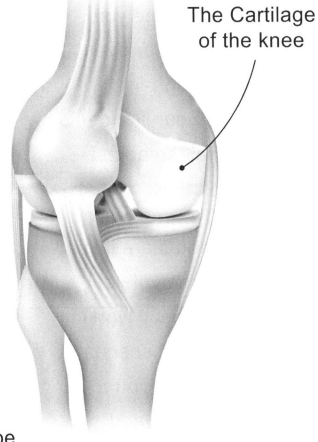

The Cartilage of the knee

Behold, the cartilage! It's like a magical cushion, a secret protector that hides in plain sight. This remarkable tissue can be found in your ears, your nose, and even in your knees. It's tough yet flexible, just like a superhero's shield.

Whenever you jump, run, or bounce, the cartilage leaps into action. It's like having your very own spring-loaded trampoline inside you! This incredible

tissue absorbs shock and protects your bones from getting hurt.

But that's not all, brave explorers! The cartilage covers the ends of your bones where they meet, like a silky coat. With its smooth surface, it allows your bones to glide together effortlessly, like a pair of dancers gracefully twirling.

Did you know that your ears are made of cartilage? That's why they can bend! It's like having a super flexible material in your body!

Did you know that the tip of our nose is made of cartilage too? It's soft and flexible, allowing us to scrunch up our noses or give Eskimo kisses without any discomfort.

So, dear young adventurers, let us salute the mighty cartilage! It's a silent hero, protecting and supporting us from head to toe. Remember, the next time you take a leap or wiggle your nose, thank the incredible cartilage, your body's hidden champion.

~ The Lungs ~

Beneath the ribcage, nestled safely in your chest, lie the magnificent lungs! Like fluffy, pink balloons, they help you breathe and give you the power to explore the world around you.

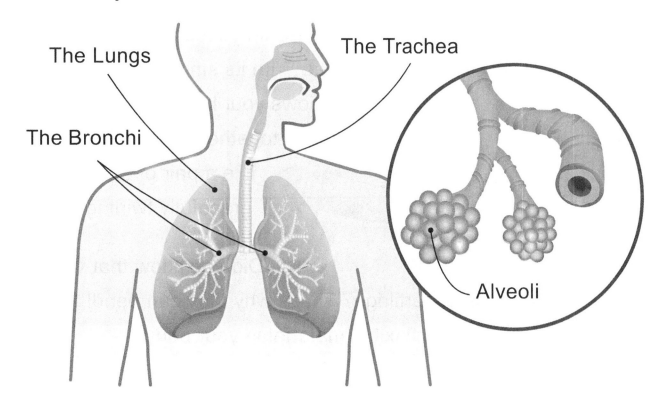

The Lungs

The Trachea

The Bronchi

Alveoli

Imagine you're climbing up a tall mountain, with the wind howling and the air thinning. As you go higher and higher, your lungs become superheroes, ready to save the day. They take in the air and deliver it to every part of your body.

Inside your lungs, there is a whole kingdom of tiny tubes called bronchi. They stretch and twist, branching out like a maze. At the end of these winding tunnels, you'll find the alveoli, which are like little pockets. There are millions of them, and they look like tiny bunches of grapes!

When you breathe in, the air rushes through your nose or mouth, down the windpipe, and into your lungs. The alveoli catch the oxygen from the air and send it straight into your blood, making it all red and full of life. At the same time, they collect the waste, like carbon dioxide, and carry it out of your body when you breathe out.

Your lungs are like two superheroes working together, always making sure you have the energy to run, jump, and play. So, take a deep breath and feel the power of your incredible lungs!

~ The Trachea ~

In the land of your body, where adventure awaits, there lies a magnificent pathway known as the trachea. It's like a secret tunnel, hidden beneath your throat, ready to guide the air you breathe!

The trachea is a brave defender, always standing tall and firm. It's made of strong rings, like a knight's armor, protecting the precious airway within. With each breath, the trachea welcomes the air in and leads it down a marvelous journey.

The Trachea

The Lungs

Imagine walking through a grand forest of your body. As you take a deep breath, the trachea opens wide, inviting the air to join its exciting expedition. Like a magical whistle, it carries the air deep into your lungs, where oxygen dances with your blood.

But beware, young explorers! The trachea faces dangers

too. Sometimes, tiny invaders called germs try to sneak in. But fear not, for the trachea has a cunning trick. It sends out tiny hairs called cilia, waving like brave warriors, to catch those pesky germs and sweep them away!

So remember, dear friends, your trachea is a mighty guardian, ensuring each breath you take is a safe and joyful one. It lets the air rush in, bringing life to every cell in your body.

How incredible it is to have such a courageous companion, protecting your breath on this grand adventure of life!

~ Yawns ~

Let's embark on an extraordinary adventure into the realm of yawns! It's a thrilling journey that reveals the magical wonders of the human body.

Have you ever felt that irresistible urge to take a big, deep breath? That's yawns!

But why do we yawn? Yawns are like a secret message from our body, telling us something important.

When we yawn, our lungs take in a huge gulp of air. This air travels through a special passage called the trachea, which leads straight to our lungs. Inside our lungs, tiny air sacs called alveoli welcome the fresh air, while old, tired air escapes.

But wait! Yawns aren't just about oxygen. They also have a special job—cooling down our brain! When we yawn, our body sends more blood to the brain, giving it a boost of energy and making us feel more alert.

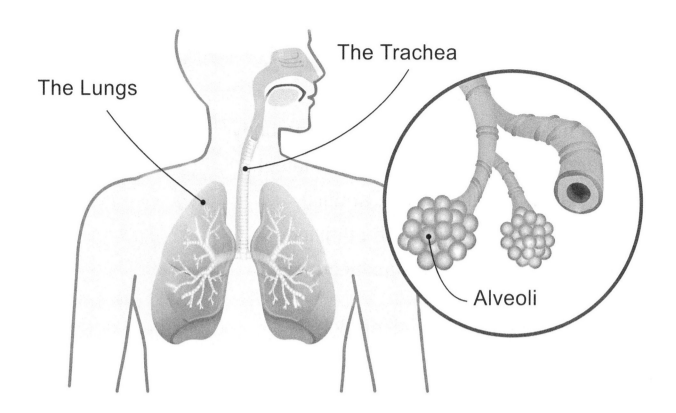

The Lungs

The Trachea

Alveoli

Yawning is contagious, too! If you see someone yawn, your brain might send you a signal to yawn as well. It's like a secret handshake between friends.

Now, here's an amazing fact: scientists still don't fully understand why we yawn. Some think it helps us communicate with others, while others believe it helps stretch our facial muscles. It's a mystery waiting to be unraveled!

~ Hiccups ~

In a hidden corner of your amazing body, there's an organ with a peculiar talent. It's called the diaphragm, and it's the mastermind behind the thrilling phenomenon we know as hiccups!

Imagine a tightrope walker high above a bustling circus. Just like that, the diaphragm rests beneath your lungs, ready to perform its incredible acrobatics.

With every breath you take, this special muscle swoops down, helping you inhale and fill your lungs with fresh air. But sometimes, the diaphragm gets a mischievous itch and decides to play a prank on you.

When the diaphragm becomes tickled or irritated, it contracts abruptly. This quick contraction catches your breath off guard, causing a hiccup. It's like a mini-explosion of air escaping from your body, making a unique sound.

Hiccups can be triggered by exciting things like eating too fast or laughing a lot.

They are harmless and usually go away on their own, but they can make us jump and giggle too!

So, next time you feel a hiccup sneaking up, remember it's just your playful diaphragm showing off its skills. Take a deep breath, let out a little hiccup, and continue enjoying the incredible adventure of your body!

~ The Liver ~

In a world of wonder, there is a remarkable organ called the liver. Nestled just beneath your ribs on the right side of your body, it works tirelessly, day and night, like a brave superhero protecting you from harm.

The Liver

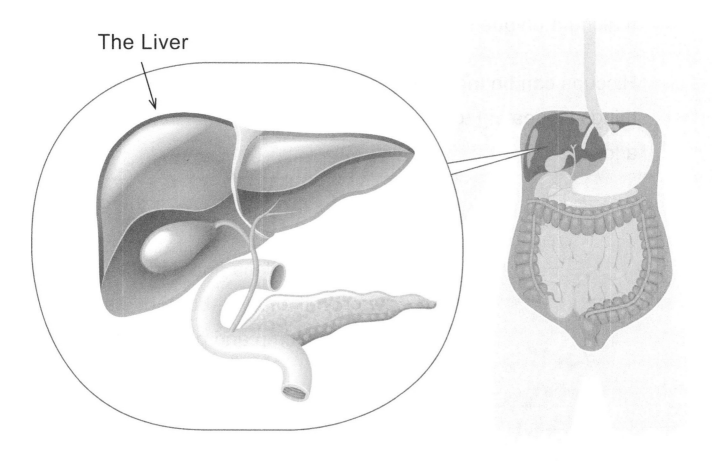

The liver is like a factory, always busy making things your body needs to stay healthy. It filters the blood that flows through it, like a brave knight guarding a castle gate, making sure only the good stuff gets in. It helps remove harmful toxins, like a secret detective on a mission to keep you safe.

But that's not all! The liver is also a master chemist. It creates a special liquid called bile, which helps your body break down the food you eat. It's like a magical potion that helps turn your food into energy, giving you the power to run, jump, and play.

Sometimes, when you eat too many sugary treats or drink too much soda, the liver can get a little overwhelmed. But fear not! It has a secret power of regeneration. Just like a superhero healing from a battle, the liver can repair itself and keep working hard.

So, next time you feel a tummy ache, remember your amazing liver. It's always there, protecting you, filtering your blood, and creating magic potions to keep you strong. Take care of it by eating healthy foods and drinking lots of water!

~ The Gallbladder ~

In a bustling city within your body, where hardworking organs tirelessly toil, there lies a gallbladder, a true hero of the human body! Imagine a tiny pear-shaped warrior, tucked beneath the liver's protective wing.

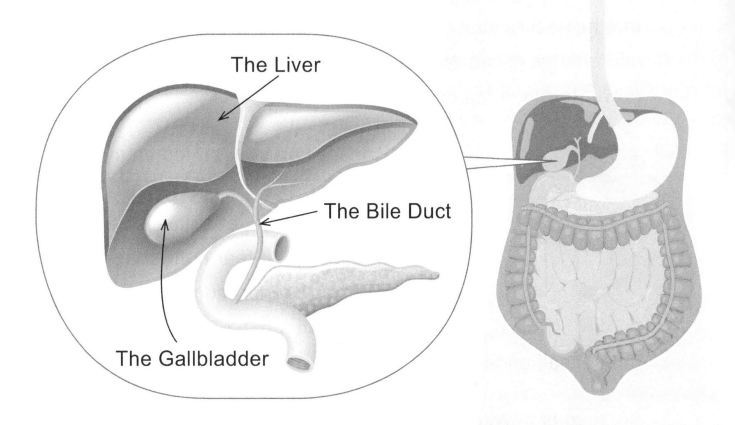

With a daring purpose, the gallbladder acts as a storage house, collecting and preserving a special liquid known as bile. Bile is like a magical potion that helps digest the food we eat, especially fatty foods. When food enters the stomach, the gallbladder senses the call to action.

Like a secret agent, the gallbladder releases the stored

bile into a winding pathway called the bile duct. It swiftly journeys to the small intestine, where it works its magic. The gallbladder's bile breaks down fats into smaller pieces, making it easier for the body to absorb nutrients and stay strong.

Sometimes, however, the gallbladder can cause trouble. It might develop tiny stones that block the pathway, causing discomfort. But fear not, brave reader, for medical wizards can help remove the gallbladder without affecting the body's power!

So next time you enjoy a tasty meal, remember to thank the gallbladder, your body's silent champion. It fights for your digestion, keeping you healthy and strong.

~ The Pancreas ~

In the bustling city of your body, there is a remarkable organ called the pancreas. Like a superhero hidden in plain sight, the pancreas has a vital mission. It stands tall, nestled snugly behind your stomach, working tirelessly to keep you healthy.

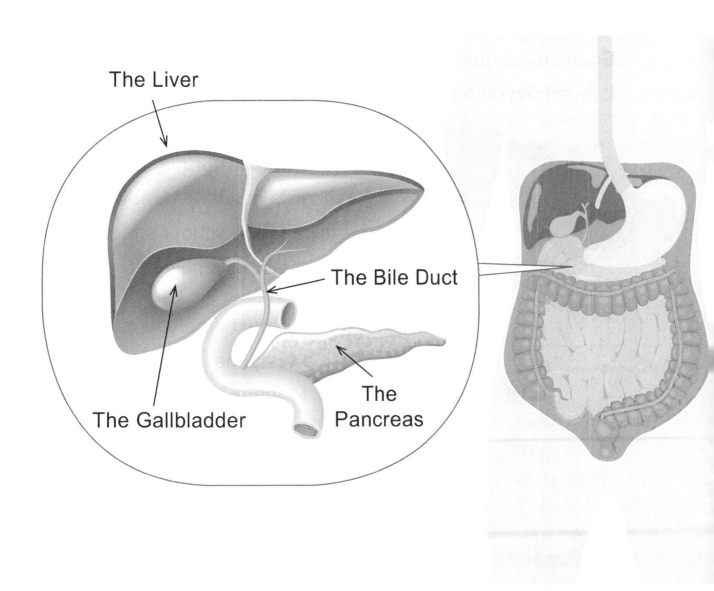

The Liver

The Bile Duct

The Gallbladder

The Pancreas

Imagine the pancreas as a clever chef in a secret kitchen, responsible for making a very special sauce called insulin. This incredible sauce helps control the amount of sugar in your body. Just like magic, the pancreas carefully measures the sugar levels, ensuring they are just right.

But wait, there's more! The pancreas doesn't stop there. It also produces another sauce called enzymes. These enzymes are like tiny superheroes that help your body break down food into smaller pieces. They work together with other organs to make sure your body gets all the nutrients it needs.

So, next time you enjoy a delicious meal, remember to thank your pancreas for its incredible work behind the scenes. It's always there, keeping an eye on your sugar levels and ensuring your body stays fueled and healthy.

The pancreas might not wear a cape or leap tall buildings, but it's a true hero inside you, protecting and nourishing you every single day.

~ The Kidneys ~

In a land within your body, where blood flows like a river, there lies a pair of incredible organs called the kidneys. They may not wear capes or fly through the sky, but their power is unmatched!

Located just below your ribs, one on each side, the kidneys are like two mighty filters. They work day and night, tirelessly removing waste and extra water from your blood, like magical cleaners.

The Kidneys

Imagine a bustling city with busy streets. Your body is like that city, and the kidneys are the skilled janitors, making sure everything stays clean and tidy. They take the impurities from your blood, leaving it fresh and pure, just like a sparkling river.

But the kidneys have another superpower! They help control the water levels in your body. When you drink lots of water, they release more, and when you're thirsty, they save water for you, like a clever reservoir manager.

Remember, the kidneys are your body's superheroes, always working silently to keep you healthy and strong. So, take care of them by drinking plenty of water and eating healthy foods. They will reward you with their amazing powers, and you'll feel as mighty as a superhero yourself!

~ The Bladder ~

In a magnificent kingdom within your body, nestled just below your belly button, resides a brave and wondrous organ called the Bladder! It's like a special reservoir that holds a magical liquid known as urine. You may also hear people use the word "pee" to describe urine.

But before the bladder can do its important job, let's talk about two other heroes in this adventure—the kidneys and the ureters. Deep within your body, the kidneys are like little factories that work tirelessly to filter your blood. They remove the extra water and waste from your body and turn them into urine.

Once the kidneys have worked their magic and created urine, the urine travels through two small tubes called ureters. The kidneys and the ureters make sure that the urine reaches the bladder safely and without any spills along the way.

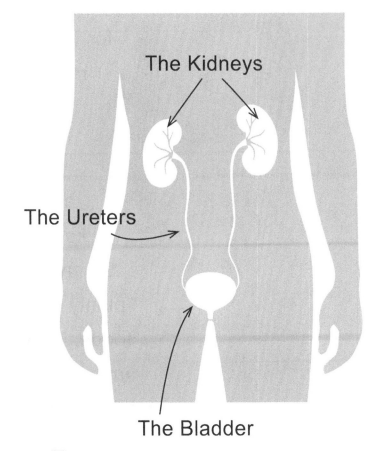

The Kidneys

The Ureters

The Bladder

When the bladder starts to fill up, it sends signals to your brain, signaling the need for a bathroom adventure. You may feel a ticklish sensation, telling you it's time to find a restroom nearby. The bladder holds your urine securely, ensuring it won't leak until you reach the right place.

Once you arrive at the restroom, the bladder becomes an ally of great strength. With a powerful squeeze, it empties the urine through a special passage called the urethra. Just like a waterfall, the urine rushes out, leaving the bladder ready for its next treasure-hunting mission.

So, next time you feel the urge to go, thank your brave bladder for being a loyal friend on this exciting journey within your body!

~ The Spleen ~

In a secret place, nestled just below your ribs, there is an extraordinary organ called the spleen. It may not be as famous as your heart or as chatty as your mouth, but the spleen has a super important job that will leave you amazed!

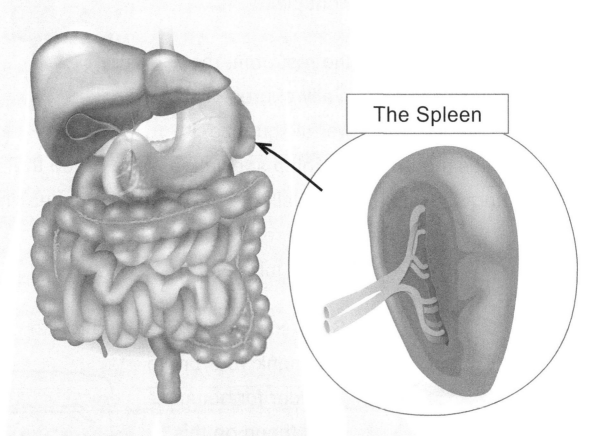

The Spleen

The spleen is like a superhero defender. It fights against icky invaders that try to make you sick. It is like a fortress, protecting your body from the sneaky germs that want to cause trouble. With the help of its trusty sidekick, the immune system, the spleen hunts down and captures the bad guys.

The spleen is also a recycling champ. It takes old and worn-out blood cells and gives them a magical makeover. It transforms them into fresh and new cells that are ready to keep you healthy and full of energy!

Imagine, right here inside your body, this brave organ is always on the lookout for trouble, defending you day and night. It never takes a break!

The spleen may be small, but it's a mighty hero that plays a big role in your amazing body. Take good care of it by eating healthy foods and getting plenty of rest, and your spleen will continue to be your trusty ally in the adventure of life!

~ The Spinal Cord ~

Located deep within the protective fortress of your spine, there exists an extraordinary treasure known as the spinal cord! This remarkable marvel resides securely within the bony tunnel formed by your vertebrae, serving as a hidden gem within your very own body.

The spinal cord is like a messenger, carrying important messages between your body and your brain. It is a long, slender cable, running from your brain down to your toes. Imagine it as a magical highway, bustling with traffic!

The Spinal Cord

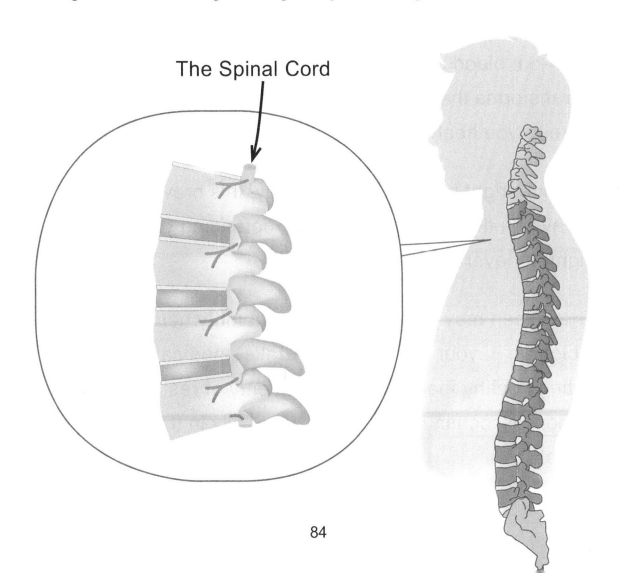

Whenever you wiggle your toes, jump, or twirl around, it's all thanks to the spinal cord. It passes on commands from your brain to different parts of your body, telling them what to do. It's like a conductor leading an orchestra, guiding the movements of your arms, legs, and even your heart.

But wait, there's more! The spinal cord is also responsible for sending messages from your body back to your brain. It acts as a superhero hotline, reporting any tickles, itches, or bumps along the way. So when you touch something hot and quickly pull your hand away, it's your spinal cord alerting your brain to the danger!

Without the spinal cord, your body would feel lost, like a ship without a compass. It is a vital guardian, ensuring that your brain and body stay connected, working together in perfect harmony.

~ The Nerves ~

In a world of sparks and signals, hidden within your amazing body, there exists a network of extraordinary messengers called nerves. They are like tiny superheroes, carrying important messages from one part of your body to another at lightning speed!

Imagine your nerves as a superhighway, buzzing with excitement. They're like the messengers of your body, delivering urgent news. When you touch something hot, your nerves shout, "Danger!" to your brain, and instantly, you pull your hand away. They keep you safe and help you feel the world around you.

Nerves are everywhere, like hidden detectives. Some nerves help you taste your favorite ice cream, while others let you see the world in all its colorful glory. They even let you feel the softness of a cuddly teddy bear or hear the cheerful melody of your favorite song.

But how do these incredible messengers work? Picture them as tiny wires, just like the ones connecting your toys. Except, instead of electricity, nerves use special signals called "impulses." These impulses zoom along the nerve highways, traveling faster than the speed of a racing car!

So, the next time you wiggle your toes or give a warm hug, remember to thank your amazing nerves. They are the true superheroes inside your body, always ready to help you explore, discover, and experience the wonders of the world!

87

~ The Esophagus ~

In a land of adventure, inside your amazing body, there is a fearless hero known as the Esophagus! Brave and strong, the Esophagus has an important mission: to transport food from your mouth to your tummy.

Picture a long, winding slide, just like the ones you love to zoom down. The Esophagus is like that slide, but hidden inside you!

When you take a big bite of yummy food, the Esophagus swings into action. It squeezes and contracts, creating a thrilling wave-like motion called peristalsis. It's like a roller coaster ride for your food!

As the food travels through the Esophagus, it's protected by a special coating of slippery mucus. This magical mucus helps the food slide smoothly, just like a water slide covered in slime. No bumps or obstacles can stop the Esophagus from completing its daring mission!

Our courageous hero knows exactly where to go. It leads the food down, down, down, and guides it safely to your tummy. Along the way, the Esophagus passes by your heart, but there's no need to worry! The Esophagus is well-trained and knows how to stay clear of trouble.

So next time you enjoy a delicious meal, remember the brave Esophagus, fearlessly delivering your food to the right place. Keep exploring the wonders of your body, and remember to give a big thank you to the incredible Esophagus!

The Esophagus

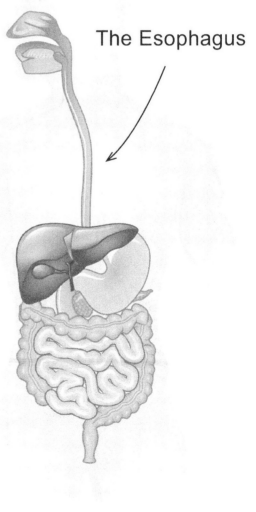

~ The Stomach ~

Deep inside your body, hidden behind your ribs and below your heart, lies a remarkable organ called the stomach. It may not seem like much from the outside, but inside, it's a world of excitement and adventure!

The stomach has an important job - it's like a big, strong mixing machine that helps us break down the food we eat. When you take a bite of that delicious sandwich or chew on a crispy apple, the stomach gets to work.

As the food enters the stomach, it starts churning and swirling around like a swirling tornado. The stomach uses its special powers to squeeze and squish the food, breaking it into tiny pieces. It

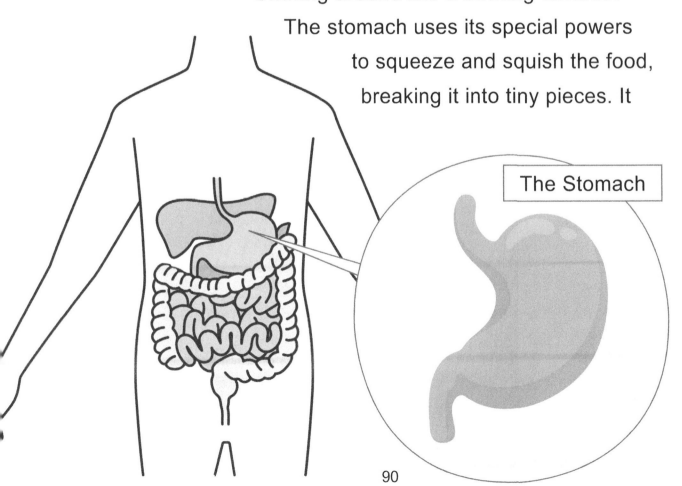

The Stomach

adds powerful juices, like a secret potion, to help dissolve the food into a soft mush.

But that's not all! The stomach has an incredible sense of time. It knows exactly when to release the mushed-up food into the next part of our body, called the small intestine. It carefully controls the flow, like a gatekeeper, making sure everything happens at the right moment.

Sometimes, the stomach gets upset or feels queasy. This can happen if we eat too quickly or eat something that doesn't agree with us. But worry not, little adventurers! The stomach is resilient and will work hard to make us feel better.

So, next time you take a bite of your favorite snack, remember to thank your marvelous stomach. It's a true hero, always ready to digest and help keep us strong and healthy.

~ The Intestines ~

In the bustling world of your body, there lies a hidden hero known as the Intestines! These amazing organs are like winding tunnels that stretch for miles, weaving through your belly. They are like the explorers of your digestive system, helping to break down and absorb the nutrients from your food.

Imagine a thrilling adventure where food enters the stomach and is turned into a mushy mixture. But wait, there's more! The Intestines step in to continue the journey. They are like long tubes, divided into two parts: the small intestine and the large intestine.

The small intestine, like a busy marketplace, is where the magic happens. It soaks up the good stuff from your food and sends it into

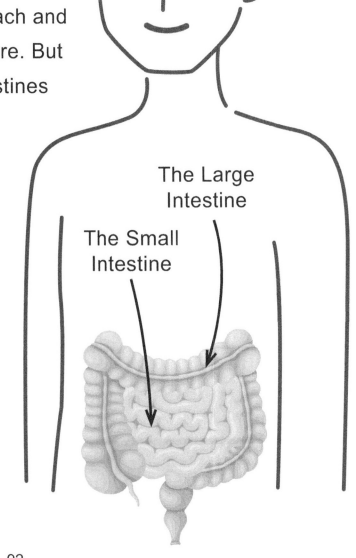

The Large Intestine

The Small Intestine

your bloodstream, giving you the energy to play and grow. The large intestine, on the other hand, is like a recycling center. It absorbs the water and gets rid of the waste that your body no longer needs.

But the Intestines have a secret power! They are covered in tiny, finger-like projections called villi. These villi grab onto the nutrients, like little superheroes, and deliver them to your body's cells.

So next time you enjoy a delicious meal, remember to thank your Intestines. They work tirelessly, ensuring you have the energy to run, jump, and explore the world around you. They truly are the heroes of your amazing body!

~ Feces ~

In a secret place, hidden within your body, something incredible happens. It's a thrilling tale about an important part of your body called "feces," or as kids often call them, "poo." Let's dive into this exciting adventure!

Every time you eat yummy food, your body works hard to take out all the useful stuff it needs. But what about the leftovers? That's where our heroes, the feces, come into play. They are like the brave warriors of your body, helping to clean up the mess!

Deep within your digestive system, the journey of the feces begins. As the food travels through your tummy, all the nutrients get absorbed, leaving behind waste that needs to be eliminated. This waste is transformed into our magical heroes!

Feces are made up of things your body can't use, like undigested food and dead cells. They gather in a special place called the large intestine, where water is taken out, making them a bit drier and more solid. Finally, when the time is right, they are ready to be released from your body.

When you feel the urge to go to the bathroom, it's your body's way of telling you that it's time to let go of them. They make their way through the small tube called the rectum and say goodbye to your body as you flush them away.

Did you know that feces can be used to make something called compost? Compost is like magic food for the soil! It helps plants grow big and strong by giving them important nutrients they need to be healthy.

So even though feces might seem yucky, they can help plants grow and make our gardens happy!

~ DNA ~

DNA is like a special instruction manual that tells our bodies how to grow and work. Just like a recipe book for making our bodies!

DNA, short for deoxyribonucleic acid, is made up of tiny building blocks called "letters." DNA uses four special letters: A, T, G, and C. They're like the alphabet of our bodies!

Did you know that DNA is shaped like a twisting ladder? Scientists call it a double helix. It's like a very cool spiral staircase that holds all the information about how our bodies should look and function.

Every person's DNA is unique, just like a fingerprint. That's why we all have different eye colors, hair types, and even talents.

But where does DNA come from? It's like a special gift passed down from your mom and dad. They each give you half of their DNA, creating a brand-new recipe just for you!

Sometimes, DNA can have little mistakes called mutations. These mutations can make us different in special ways. For example, they can make some people have curly hair while others have straight hair. It's what makes us all wonderfully unique!

DNA doesn't just belong to humans. Every living thing, like plants and animals, also has DNA. It's like a secret language that all living creatures use to grow and survive.

~ Hormones ~

Hormones are special chemicals in our bodies that act like messengers. They help different parts of our body communicate and work together, just like friends passing notes! They have special powers to change our emotions and moods.

Hormones can also help our bodies react quickly in emergencies. When we get scared or need to run fast, a hormone called "adrenaline" gives us a burst of energy and makes our hearts beat faster. It's like having a real-life superpower!

One famous hormone is called "oxytocin." It's known as the "love hormone" because it makes us feel warm and fuzzy when we hug someone we care about, like our family or friends. So, the next time you feel a big hug, remember it's the love hormone at work!

Another hormone is called "melatonin." It's like a sleepy superhero that helps us fall asleep at night and wake up in the morning. So when you feel tired at bedtime, remember it's melatonin doing its nighttime job!

Remember, hormones are like little messengers that help our bodies do amazing things. They're always working behind the scenes, just like superheroes, to keep us happy and healthy.

~ The Male ~
Reproductive System

In a land of wonder and adventure, there exists an extraordinary set of organs known as the male reproductive system. This remarkable system holds the key to creating new life. Let's embark on a thrilling journey to uncover its secrets!

Between the legs of men, there is a special place called the testes. Here, something special is made called sperm. These tiny superheroes are so small you need a microscope to see them. Their mission is to join forces with a very special egg, known as mummy's egg, and start a new human being.

The testes create spermatozoa, incredible cells with long tails that help them swim. These brave explorers travel through tiny tubes called the vas deferens.

But before they can fulfill their mission, they receive an important addition from the prostate gland, a special organ that adds a sticky liquid to the sperm. This liquid provides them with energy and protection for their upcoming journey.

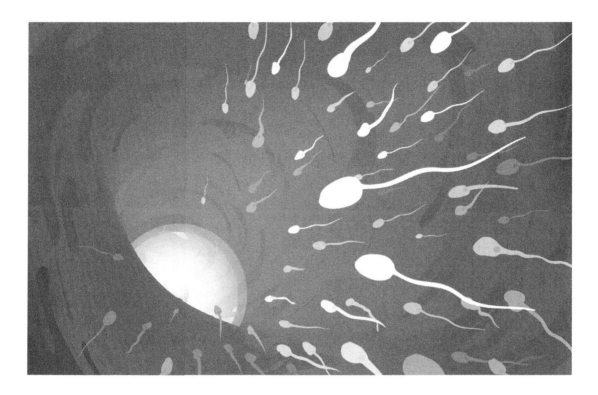

After their adventurous journey, the spermatozoa reach the egg. In a thrilling race, they compete to be the first to reach it. The fastest and strongest spermatozoa become the lucky winners and unite with mummy's egg to create a tiny baby.
This incredible process is called fertilization.

And that's how mummy's pregnancy starts!

~ The Female ~
Reproductive System

In a hidden part of a special place called the female body, there's an incredible and magical system called the female reproductive system. It has a crucial job: to help create new life. Let's explore its fascinating functions!

Inside the female body, there is a small, butterfly-shaped organ called the uterus. The uterus is like a cozy home for a tiny baby. Every month, it gets ready to welcome a special visitor called an egg. The egg is the start of a new life!

In another special place called the ovaries, there are lots of tiny eggs, waiting patiently for their turn. These eggs are called ova or oocytes. Every month, one egg leaves the ovary and travels through a tiny tube called the fallopian tube.

Now, here comes the most exciting part! If a friendly visitor called sperm meets the egg in the fallopian tube, something incredible happens. The sperm and egg join together, like puzzle pieces fitting perfectly. This is called fertilization, and it's the beginning of pregnancy.

It's like a magical adventure happening right inside a mummy's body. And each one of us started our journey here!

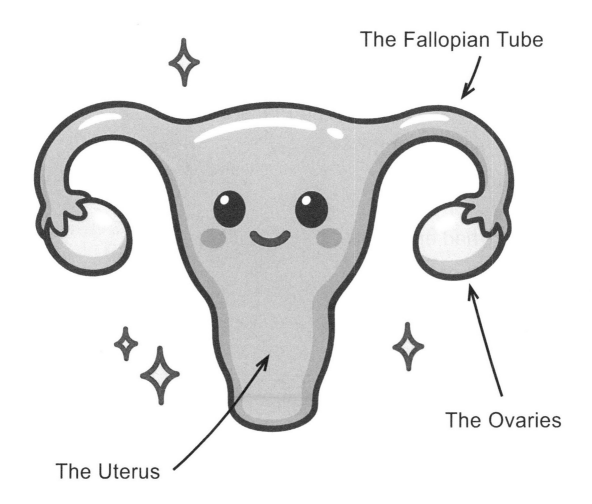

The Fallopian Tube

The Uterus

The Ovaries

~ Pregnancy ~

Once upon a time, in a mommy's tummy, something magical happened. It all began when a tiny, special sperm met a tiny egg, starting an incredible adventure called fertilization. When these two tiny friends joined together, they created the spark of life, beginning the amazing journey of pregnancy.

Inside the mommy's tummy, the fertilized egg grew into a tiny, growing baby. It started as an embryo, smaller than a pea, and soon became a fetus. The fetus floated in a cozy, watery world called the amniotic sac, which was like a special, protective bubble. This sac kept the baby safe, warm, and snug.

The baby had another special helper called the placenta. The placenta was like a magical bridge that connected the baby to the mommy. It acted like a food delivery

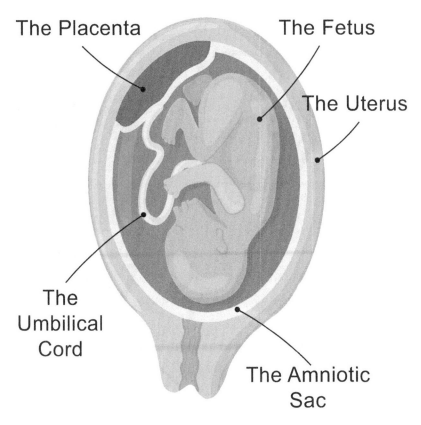

The Placenta

The Fetus

The Uterus

The Umbilical Cord

The Amniotic Sac

system, bringing yummy nutrients and oxygen from the mommy's body to the baby through a special cord called the umbilical cord.

Fetal development

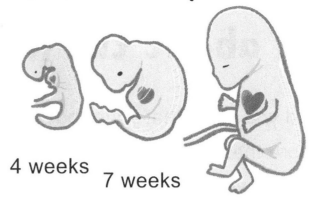

4 weeks

7 weeks

12 weeks

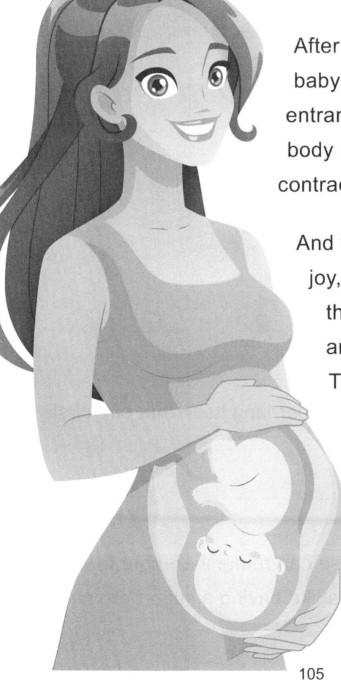

After nine months, the baby was ready for a grand entrance. The mommy's body prepared for birth, and contractions began.

And finally, with a burst of joy, the baby arrived, filling the world with laughter and tears of happiness. The journey of pregnancy was remarkable, where a tiny seed grew into a beautiful baby, creating a bond between mommy, daddy, and child that lasts forever.

~ Amazing Facts ~ about the Human Body

Did you know that your body has more than 600 muscles? They help you move, jump, dance, and do all sorts of fun things like a flexible superhero!

Did you know that if you stretched out all the blood vessels in your body, they would go around the Earth more than twice? That's like having a super long hose that can circle the whole planet!

Did you know that your nose can remember more than 50,000 different smells? It's like having a superhero sense that helps you enjoy the sweet scent of flowers or the delicious aroma of fresh-baked cookies.

Your body has a natural built-in clock called a circadian rhythm. It helps you know when it's time to sleep, wake up, and do all the fun things throughout the day.

Your hair is super strong, even though it looks soft and delicate. If you gathered all the hairs on your head and tied them together, they could hold the weight of two elephants!

Your taste buds can change every few weeks. That's why you might start liking foods you didn't enjoy before. It's like having taste buds with the power to evolve!

The strongest bone in your body is the femur, which is as strong as steel! It's the bone in your thigh and can support your whole body weight, like a superhero's unbreakable leg.

Your body is made up of trillions of cells, just like the stars in the sky. They work together like a team of superheroes to keep you healthy and strong.

Your body has a powerful natural defense system called the immune system. It fights off germs and keeps you healthy, like a shield-wielding superhero protecting you from villains.

The acid in your stomach is strong enough to dissolve metal! It helps break down the food you eat into tiny pieces so your body can absorb all the good stuff.

Did you know that your body is taller in the morning than at night? When you sleep, the discs in your spine get a chance to rest and expand, making you a little taller when you wake up.

Your body is constantly making new skin cells. In fact, every month, you get a completely new outer layer of skin. It's like having a fresh superhero suit all the time!

Did you know that your body is mostly made up of water? More than half of you is made up of this amazing liquid that helps keep you hydrated and healthy.

Educa' Fun

Made in the USA
Las Vegas, NV
13 October 2023

79045888R00063